Stomp Your Boots With Some Vigor

Tara Sparbel

Front Cover Design by: Avalon Clare Illustration

Cover Art: Self Portrait by Anne Germain

For:

Mom
Papa

Anne Germain
Annie Greylak
Luke Rudolph

I.   Stargazer

II.   Gentleman's Waistcoat Pocket

III. Zog Zag Teeth

IV. Burnt Sienna Mouth

I.

Stargazer

WHIPPERSNAPPER

In someone else's story I'm the bully on the bus
I don't remember being the bully on the bus
But she remembers me as the bully on the bus
I'll always be the bully on the bus, to her
In someone else's story I'm the sound
of vomiting the next stall over
at a dive bar and she's saying
"Is everything okay?"
To a stall,
I'll always be the person
She never wants to be, to her

In someone else's story I'm the one
who got away
In someone else's story I'm the one
who didn't respond
In someone else's story
I'm the friend who stabbed them
in the back
In someone else's story
I'm the baby who smiled back
at them in the grocery store
and brought them back to life
They remember that day fondly

In someone else's story
I'm forever seventeen

In someone else's story
I'm the Villain,
the car nose picker,
the grumpy
clerk at check out
To them, I will always be the grumpy
clerk at checkout

In someone else's story
I remain pressed between the
pages of their journal with a sprig
of lavender
In someone else's story I
remind them of someone,
but dammit they can't
place it

A Vagabond

In someone else's story I was the
best thing that ever happened to them
In someone else's story I was the
worst thing that ever happened to them
I gave the best, worst, welcomed, and
unwarranted advice
In someone else's story
I'm the Eavesdropper
just out of focus
in the restaurant
when the big news
was revealed
In someone else's story
I've got it all
In someone else's story
I've got a lot to learn

In someone else's story
I'm the Teacher, Prophet,
Sign They've Been Waiting For,
The Daydreamer, Protagonist,
Antagonist, Sidekick, Skeptic, Mentor,
Tempter, Bitch, Subject of Interrogation

In someone else's story I'm the
Grave Digger, Caretaker, Smoker,
Organ Donor, Sucker, Slowpoke,
Tourist, Whippersnapper, Secret Keeper,
Impostor, Stargazer, Chicken,
Duuude

In someone else's story
I'm the girl who stole the
art books
I didn't steal the art books
I'd say it's out of my character,
but in their story
I'll always be that character:
A Liar
and a Thief

In someone else's story
they looked away moments
before I entered the scene
They were too busy
Digging dirt from their fingernails
Brushing hair out of their eyes
Staring down at their feet
Checking their phone
I remain the whisper
they hear when they turn
the page
or open a door

In someone else's story
I'm the girl the next page over
The next page over
The next page over
They keep flipping,
but the plot
has thickened and I'm

trapped in their tattered
binding, lips red from
the paper cut of the bookmark
they place so frequently
but never return to

In someone else's story
they jump right over me
to the conclusion

In someone else's story
they mouth the words
"The End" and I ask
"Can you tell it again?"
And I hang on every word
The cat that got their tongue
and made it purr

In someone else's story
I cease to exist at all

But then,
I'm the stubborn red lipstick
dried to the lip of the tea cup
They scrub and scrub,
but can't erase me
A kiss frozen in time
An ember that ignites
a memory

ASCEND

She's aged
ten years
in the last year
You don't see it
in her face
You hear it
in her voice
Which is
sharp
and bitter
When she
opens her
mouth to
speak her
tongue sticks
to her teeth
She says
she'd rather
walk twelve
flights of stairs
than
board an elevator
with a man she
doesn't know

THEY'LL

Never
know
the
curves
of
your
face
tears
linger
longest

CEREMONY

For once when someone
asks how I am doing
I would like to pause
Lay down wherever I may be
Fingers laced over my soft belly
Feet crossed at the ankles
Hair spread like a halo
And tell them:
Well Darling,

...the most sacred place I have been...
...the second time I fell in love...
...my third non-negotiable is...
...when I can't sleep at night I...
...I learned this lesson the hard way...
...the big dipper was his favorite constellation...
...and grandma smoked for years, when we took the Last
Supper painting off her wall...
...was miles from town, broke down, blizzard...
...he did this seemingly for no reason at all...
...pulling each strand of hair out one by one...
...running down the sand dunes full speed...
...i never spoke with her again after that...
...he flicked a cigarette in her face...
...slowest shooting star I had ever seen...
...my biggest fear is...
...and it was a ceremonial occasion...
...ate his own bed sheets...
...i dreamt it over and over...
...page 328 line 4 really speaks volumes...
...and he said "light on your feet!"...
...open air funeral in the desert mountains...
...I was never the same after that...

But instead I adjust my coat tighter
And say "Brr."
As my story trails behind me
like a loose-knit, tongue-tied scarf
Vowels chewed off the inside of my cheeks
Consonants lost in the wind

TIMES WE SIGH

As we slink into eucalyptus bath
A heavy breath escapes us suddenly
After a weightful, satisfying meal
You got the job
You lost the job
You quit the job
The pregnancy test is negative
The pregnancy test is positive
Injustice
Orgasms
You haven't danced in years
You dance
Rest your head on a shoulder
The flight takes off
The flight lands
Election results
Test results
Medical exam results
The cat jumps in your lap
A heave of relief, a ho of exhaustion
Grief
Satisfaction
You made it just in time
Found the last bit of cinnamon in the spice cabinet
Touchdown
Aunt flo, I thought you'd never come
Aunt flo, how could you
Your timing is a mess
A kiss
Last page of a book
Whiff of lavender
Clean house, messy house, new house, no house, moving
Moving on
That sunny, warm car feeling in Spring

Rest your head on the dog's belly
Disappointment
Alone again
Together again
Alone at last
Together at last
Put on the spot
When
There's nothing left to say

TIMES WE GASP

Ladder falls
Baby stands
Toddler falls
Standing under
Water falls
Lights go out
Stage lights turn on
Glass slips
Glass drops
Glass shatters
Ball drops
Hope shatters
Bird meets window
Jumping in
Jumping out
Red stains, white panties
White panties
Blood
Cold blood, Hot blood
Diamond ring
Spattering
Gaspy breath
Singing singing
When there's nothing you can say

TIMES YOU SHOULDN'T TALK TO ME

Cervix is open
Legs in stirrups
Stirring oatmeal
Goshdarn cursing
News unnerving
Eyes averting
Pairing socks
Untangling knots
Dark parking lots
Voting polls
Over stalls
Under stalls
Through the door
Through the walls
Solo walk
Dental impressions
Walgreens
Baking sessions
Elevators
Ever

RUBE GOLDBERG MACHINE

I imagine Grief
as tiny gold coins
that form every time
you muster strength
or courage through
dark times
and stored in a treasure
chest, no not in your chest,
but in some heavy crevice
just below your belly button

And sometimes it takes
just one word, to set off
the domino effect,
the release of currency
that has sunk somewhere
in the sands of your gut

Yeah, that's that sinking feeling

The pendulum swings
and releases the knife that
cuts the bag of sedimentary rocks
that's been hovering above your chest
since you-know-when

The piano key is struck
and your vocal chords
release the ancestral groan
that's been writing poetry
on shore with a stick,
but it's been washed away
too many times

The marble reaches that space
behind your eyes
that drips dark like a wet cave
of gypsum crystals
It breaks the levy and your face is wet

But your eyes sparkle again
like two milky pearls
spit from the tongue of the clam
that's kept them from seeing the light

PIROUETTES

When we were young
we prayed to a god
we were convinced existed

Now we pray to Pirouettes,
our own Beating Heart,
the Blood Moon,
Star Constellations,
and every form of
Precipitation

It doesn't feel any different
The language is the same

Godly Gasps and Bone Shrines
Rosaries and Blood Lines
Inner Goddess
Feline
Pharaohs, Monks,
And Crystalline
Prayers to Pirouettes
to Pirouettes to Pirouettes
to Pirouettes

SURFSIDE 7

Your smiles changed
you're a woman now

   I liked you from a distance
but what happened to you
   here in front of me

Your smiles changed

STARFRECKLES

I saw it at the thrift store
Couldn't leave without it
Gathered change in the car
to buy it
Now it sits at the bottom of the closet
wrinkled and abandoned
after one guest appearance on instagram

Phases of the moon on a baseball tee

How immortal, how worldly, will pair
nicely with high waisted jeans
Black lipstick
Now everyone will know how I
rise and fall with the tides

Or it, at least, implies

I know the man on the moon
He brings monthly red roses, dripping
He writes wicked sonnets
He sheds light on secrets we've kept
in the dark

But mostly: He mocks us

Tips his hat and
plays the flute while we run our fingers
along metal fences

Starfreckles
Kerosene constellations

We've wished on every one

How we rise and how we burn out
from time to time
How we search and how we buy
How we are always left
wanting
more

FLORAL FIXATION

I love you-
but I especially love
the way you say "no."
a mile before approaching
any velvet seventies floral print chair
sad and abandoned on
a cold cement curb
You know my affinity
for olive green orange mustard
disco loungers
Musty damp street couches
Alone and so afraid
Can't save them all
from the throes of the diva dump
But you know I try
You grab my hand as we
drive past,
"I know, darlin', I know."

DUO

me-tea and turmeric   lime seltzer   tempers swelter
documentaries and daisies

     flames   mustard battered books paraphrase she
and he- paw prints   lip prints   prince   dividends

     sea salt   kelp   honey bee   honey dew   honey
do   honey hear   honey see   you don't see- me

he- flowers   roads   rose to see mowed   roses   prick
prick   smudge   smoke   prayer   sage   sweetgrass
petals fall behind glass   beast   he
     me- dead ends   means to and end
bookends   mend   mend   wrap your head
around   comprehend that

he- hold hands   cold hands   fingers   but mostly   nails

     I- march forth   11:11   seas of the seven   clever
and brethren   moons and gods   fangs and claws   probable
cause   visionaries   sanctuaries   shrines of bone   shrines
of feather   signs of ache   ache shrines of ash

backlash

PICKING MYSELF UP OFF THE FLOOR

Starts with the head
I run my fingers underneath
my skull and smell it like
a ripe cantaloupe

It's sweet. It's ready.

Tuck my hair behind my ear
and whisper, "Darling. It's time."

Jam both my arms underneath
my armpits and lift up
But my body is so heavy

I tell her, "The dishes can wait."
And see her fingernails dance
I tell her, "You don't have to know
the answers to that right now."
And see her eyelashes flutter
I tell her, "It's time to love yourself."
She takes the fetal position

Waiting to be loved

"Time to get up!" I say to her
She pushes away the tile
Hair wild with expectations

I tell her "Everything doesn't
need to be perfect all
the time."
And
"Happiness isn't a
permanent state of mind."

And I swear to god
I watched her fly

WELL, SHOOT

At what point
does uncertainty
become productive

On our deathbed
where we are fairly
certain, it was
not productive
to spend a lifetime
reaching out
for
certainty

THIS IS ME

this is me
this me owning my calluses
this is me owning my balance
this is me owning my strut
this is me owning my stride
this is me owning my pace
this is me kicking my heels up
this is me digging my toes in
this is me pivoting pivoting
this is me i'm my support
this is me getting my footing
this is me owning my sole
this is my soul, she owns me

PLEASE

Don't try to grasp
anything I'm saying

It doesn't mean anything
Even if it means everything
to me

Hold it
loosely in the
palm of your hand
Wiggle it around
and let it slip
through your fingers

Throw it on
the ground
Watch it shatter
into a hundred
interpretations
Drop it like a cube
in spritzer and watch
it rise to the occasion

But don't hold its hand
and squeeze its slippery
palm purple

Don't hug it to your body
and stick your slick tongue
inside its ear

Don't look into its eyes
Don't hold your breath
Don't give it life

AFTER SOBRIETY

She wanted to feel
Something,
Anything
She hadn't
Felt Something,
Anything
in so long
Made a path
behind her one
bedroom home
Wisconsin forest
Walking barefoot
Blinding night
Cold mud biting
Pinecones piercing
Rock path screaming
Dead leaves clinging
Tree bark splitting
Toenails bleeding
Pain was healing
She was healing
What a feeling
She was feeling
Something,
Anything

CHAI IN CRESTONE

Every time I spoke with Paul,
he revealed something
extraordinary about himself
He new Allen Ginsberg
Built stupas, adobe homes
Oversaw an open
air cremation movement
Planted 300 trees in the valley
Spoke in poetic, spiritual,
philosophical anecdotes
I feared he would find me out
Realize I wasn't on the same
spiritual astral plane as him,
whatever that means

At five a.m. daily, I would hear
Paul meditating from his bedroom
Sing, hum, murmur
His motto:
"Out of your head, into the elements"
I had imagined him "transcending time and space"-
a term I learned watching Huckabees
Imagined him leaving his body,
floating over the San Luis Valley
swallowing clouds containing
the earthly wisdom I wasn't ready to digest

By the time I pulled myself from bed
He was completely pulled together
Barefoot in a flannel and sunhat
Homemade chai from scratch
A recipe he learned living in India

Since Crestone is home to twenty five
active spiritual centers,
Paul was quick to conclude
that you won't find inner change
following any one: religion, leader, guru
if you weren't willing to do the inner-work necessary,
"The change comes from within,
but that's what people avoid",
he'd say as he smeared a gob
of salted butter cream on his face,
"Great moisturizer!"

The next day, as I joined Paul
for breakfast,
he asked exactly what I had been
aching for,
"Do you want to know what I was
thinking about during my daily
meditation this morning?"
Yes.
"Yesterday you asked for coconut milk
in your chai,
but I used 2 percent."

Tara Sparbel

II.

Gentleman's Waistcoat Pocket

LEROY STREET

She told me,
"I used to think factory smoke
was a cloud making machine."

I recall the time
I was summoned
to the curb in front
of my childhood home
Leroy Street
Police sirens
I stood there, heavy jawed
Gap tooth grinned
Black tinted windows
A limousine, I thought

Someone important was in there

I waved until my arms were sore
Until my elbows twinged and yelped
Car after car
Small orange flags
drove by
I waved and waved
Greeted them with enthusiasm
Expected candy

A parade
On our very own street

Someone important was in there

GOOD INTENTIONS GONE WRONG

When I was ten
I'd stand by the
Win- a- Goldfish
game at the fair

Pluck all the
unwanted clear
plastic bags of
of goldfish from
the trash

Line them up
on the cement curb
next to the ferris wheel

I had imagined
a better life for them

That they would live to
be old, and greyfish

I thought I was saving
the world, but I was
just boiling goldfish
in the summer
sun

FUNHOUSE MIRROR

When they separated
He started
hunting, skinning, and eating
squirrels in the deep Wisconsin forest

And she fished out
her mouse ears
and began planning a trip
to the happiest place on earth

And I wonder:
In the face of life transition:
Who am I?
The hunter-gatherer?
Sweaty human in
a puppet suit?
The omnivore?
The muppet?
Cold feet in the stream?
Fantasia?

Or would I be somewhere
in between?

Chipping my tooth
on a bottle of rootbeer
chasing fireworks
across a baseball diamond

Soysauce
On pancakes

Peeling hard boiled eggs
on a tilt-a-whirl
Shells in a
Ball blue compost jar

Lemondrops melting
on the dashboard
in the sun

RITA WITH THE RED NAILS

Grandma got her nails done
maraschino cherry red
at the nursing home
where she resides

She tells us "Papa
will be mad"
And we walk
into the room to
find her sitting on
her hands in shame

I can't help but wonder
if Rita's short white hair
looks like long golden
locks when she looks
in the mirror

She wants the
nail polish off

She's getting ready to
see him
She's getting ready to
go home

DESTINATION: DESTINY

On my flight to Santa Cruz
I had somehow
conjured up the idea
the man next to me
would be a wise man,
a guru of sorts

He'd tell me exactly
what I needed to hear
to move forward
with noticeably new charisma
"A spark ignited within her!"
They'd say
and I'd chalk it up
to this very moment

I turned to him and said,
"The ocean! There it is!"
Expecting him to say
"The ocean becometh you,
and swallow whole your fears!"

And just like that,
I'd be released of
everything holding me back

Instead, he turned toward me,
yawned peanut breath
followed by a small,
chortled snort

GENTLEMAN'S WAISTCOAT POCKET

These holidays weigh heavy
I can see the deep sigh
of your sweet belly
as you pick up the phone
to say Happy Holidays

To someone who isn't there
To someone who hasn't been there
To someone who used to be
But now- is not

I can see the deep sigh of
your tired eyes
As you pick up the phone
Curl your lips into a smile
Spell "hello" with your
pink tongue in calligraphy

The knot of your fleshy muscle
a tangled mass of christmas lights
a rope around a package
carefully curated with nothing of value inside

These holidays are mocking
with
Mistletoe
Music meant for slow dancing
Fireside charades

You don't feel in love with
Someone who is distant
Someone who has left
Someone sitting idly by

Someone whose pursed lips
are no longer soft
Their words are
chapped from licking their wounds
too many times

These holidays weigh heavy
They don't wait for anyone
to feel better or to change
their circumstances

They exist in plain view
And tap us on the shoulder
And trip us on the sidewalk
And call us and hang up
And send us bills instead of carols
And cramps instead of fruitcake
And wet eyes instead of fireworks

No, there's no fireworks at all
Just burnt out bulbs in cardboard boxes
where loose glitter glistens from the bottom
And ornaments say 1997
And the face staring back at you
Is someone you no longer know
And you wish you could tell it so many things
And the music box is broken-

It spins in silence just like you
Spins in silence just like you
In silence just like you
Silence just like you
Just like you
Like you
You

NAUSEA

I
feel
like
I
am
going
to
grow
up
all
over
myself

CRANES

An IV drip
The saline solution makes you cold
Request a warm blanket, whiskey
from the tan leather recliner
Hot coffee, black   free dark
chocolate milano cookies from
the waiting room
The window in room 10 - a portal
to the outside: tan grass, highway
But in your restful slumber-
You are knee deep, the saline solution:
a cold stream - wool socks, waders,
fishing rod, ties you tied in the basement
of the house you built, on the bar you built
with your son
Your eyebrows raise in delight
Something wild bending your line
Stomach flutters, a rush as you reel it in
You call your loved ones, it was the biggest
fish you'd ever seen
The trees are bare, the ground - yellow, orange
I hear a heavy sigh in your sleep as
the stream c a r r i e s your worries away
The wind carries your fears
The mountains carry your burdens
You are light, You rest in joy,
You feel peace

WISDOM TEETH REMOVAL

You'll have
less teeth
so your head
will feel lighter
and your jaw
won't feel so heavy
so you'll be able
to talk twice as fast

You'll have
less teeth
so your head
will feel lighter
and your jaw
won't feel so heavy
so you'll be able
to talk twice as fast

III.

Zog Zag Teeth

MOTIVE

This poem is not meant for you
If that hurt your feelings
This poem is meant for you
If you're still reading this
This poem is meant for you
This poem is not meant for you
It's not meant for me either
It simply exists in verbiage
and son of a gunnery

It has a mustache
and a red satin dress
Because I put it there
If that hurt your feelings
This poem is not meant for you

It relates to people in soundbites
and when it gets nervous
all its letters italicize

And someday, perhaps it will exist
on paper, free from the
self conscious cursor
that worries
about blinking too much
and subsequently eats these words like
comfort food, leaving
a trail of crumbs that spell
out bad advice in a font
reminiscent of craft show
comic sans

That advice was not meant for you
But without this poem to warn you
How were you to know?

But nevermind any of that
Because
This poem was not meant for you
Unless it was meant for you
In the end
It is not the author who decides
It is you

WHAT SHOULD I TITLE THIS POEM

She asked as
she placed one
green pitted olive
on each of her ten
tuckered fingers

The olives did not answer back

So she ate them,
one by one

WRITING WITH A MIGRAINE

Wish i could say
What should be said
Instead i said say
Say said said said said

ELECTRIC RHYTHM HARD CANDY

feels like disco
down a zig zag beam
biting nails into zag zigs
with zog zag teeth
your perforated tongue
licks the mirror
scratching scars into
your reflection
eyes watering
silver glitter flicker pupil
boogie lip lick blood
sparkle glove
bump and hustle
break
icicles down from
the front entrance of your
holly jolly melt in your
mouth
sugar tooth
enamel enamored
cutie cuticles
a relationship you
hoped would end
lest you ever
have hands
meant for tickling
the back of someone you
met a week ago
lying belly down on
your bed as you discover
their sweat made into tiny
salt crystals with the flick of
your witch wrist and your
kitty cat claws

peppermint
air gusting through the window
blowing the curtains open
and frosting your cake
blue and sweet, ice cream
spoon melting as it dips
into cold milk
and claws your bones
a-shiver
electric rhythm hard candy

Tara Sparbel

AAAAAAA

I pick up a sentence from the page
and drape it across my body
like a pageant sash
Take the O and say
With this ring
I thee wed
And marry myself
on the corner
by the gas station
drinking a rootbeer float

The P makes a nice hat
when you turn it sideways
And the U is a deep, empty
pool where pine needles
and skateboarders gather
someplace in Surfboard, California
The Y makes a nice martini glass
And a martini glass makes
anything fancy

Q is balloon sent up to the heavens
K is a rewind button on an old VCR
J is an umbrella handle
I pull out the lowercase t|
when crucifying myself
or adding hot sauce to
an omelet
Many A's make a mountain range
AAAAAA
I rest here and
meet pantomiming clowns
who mine crystals on the night of the
crescent moon which looks a little like C

EAT GREEN OLIVES

Would this poem be more beautiful if
it had a different name attatched
If every line would repeat
If every line would repeat
Would this poem be more beautiful
if it sprouted from soil
sewn into the creases of an elbow
planting lines of produce
like a sonnet in the spring morning sun
Would this poem be more beautiful
if it accepted itself for spelling 'attatched'
incorrectly, would it be more beautiful if
it succumbed to the perfectionism it
has always been attached to
If it separated itself from its need to be flawless
Would this poem be more beautiful
if its form

was

        more

fucked up

and   all over   the

   place

the way it feels on dizzy weekend mornings
barefoot in the cold, wet grass
s t r e t c h i n g while the dog relieves itself
A "vowel movement"- the author laughs

Would this poem be more beautiful if it prayed to
a shrine of poets past, present, future

If it saged itself and blessed italics *holy*
If it was more **bold**
Would this poem be more beautiful

if it was more concise
Concise.
Punctuation?

     White space

Would this poem be more beautiful if it let
us read
EAT
between
GREEN
the lines
OLIVES
Would this poem be more beautiful
if it changed its name to
something outside the confines
of this poem and said things like,
"My stomach twisted like a testicle"
Or
Compared women to fruit and men
to hands and dogs to gods
Would this poem be more beautiful on a stage
Would this poem be more beautiful
in the wastebasket

Would this poem be more beautiful
if it went on forever
Or if it ended
by

J

u

m

p

i

n

g

D

O

W

N

?

IV.

Burnt Sienna Mouth

HONEYCOMB CRESCENDO

It was a butterfly funeral
Orange and black in late September
Sun dried worms wore top hats
and pocket squares in their suit coats

The black widow stuck
to the sole of a boot
brought cuban cigars
and blew smoke rings
that the fleas, full of glee,
jumped through

The dragonfly on the windshield
brought fruit salad and sage

The ladybug in the polka dot dress
smeared lipstick on the neck
of the ladybird beetle as they mourned
on a box of saltine crackers

The moth that could not resist
the candle flame burned palo
santo near a shrine of tick blood
dry and black as cat on hallows eve

The centipede wore one hundred dress shoes

It was a butterfly funeral
You see a life flash before you
The metamorphosis
From Egg
to Caterpillar
From Chrysalis
to Butterfly

It was a butterfly funeral
And as the honey bees
opened their hive
and let the tired butterfly inside
the piano played a solemn melody

Tara Sparbel

PRESERVERE

The May moon is wild
The strawberry shelves are empty
at the grocery store

EMERALD CITY FEVER FETISH

Don't worry, dear, autumn will soon arrive
with its death and its touches
with its branches and grudges
with its sawmills and cat tongues
with its unrequited love and lip lust
its gravestones and silence
with its burning embers and root vegetables
harvest moons and jars of grasshoppers

Yes, autumn will soon reach out
with its gusts of fleeting rot
with its candlelight and witch doctors
its hypnosis and thieves oil
with its spells and constellations
fortune tellers and black squirrels
with its tease of permanence
its hot liquids, webs, seances

My dear, autumn is here
with its burnt sienna mouth
And its vine and carriage tongue
Chiclet fangs and
poison ivy breath
Drowning applecheeks of blue
Its lies give us cavities

It promises maple mustard milky ways
emerald city northern lights
orchards of blood and rubies and pie
but gives us fog instead

It gives us fog instead

Tara Sparbel

WISCONSIN RIVER

I feel most like myself in the winter
When cold is biting my fingers
I cross them behind my back
and promise I'm okay

I feel most like myself in the winter
When hot broth like lava down my throat
tingles goosebumps to my feet
Dumpling cheeks steam warmth
to my carrot nose and charcoal eye

I feel most like myself in the winter
When water on its way to the ball freezes
mid-drip, we drop jaw at its dazzle,
never asking why it chose to froze
instead of fight or flight

I feel most like myself in the winter
When sun isn't guilting me through
gaps in the blinds and the neighborhood
is hushed, muffled, static, crunch
pop top kshhh ahhh with a can of coca cola

I feel most like myself in the winter
When the record player stops
and my heart echoes the pulsating crack of
ice on the river where salmon gather
for a glimpse of sky

MONK GARDENS

The best part of their day
was when their phone died
beneath a maple tree
listening to wind chimes
Frost bit soil and sunrise

The nylon strings tangled
in the wind
They thought about helping
it along, untangling it's mess
to hear its chest rise in song

As they reached their hand
toward the leaves, they
could feel their ancestors
breathe

Oak breath and Pine teeth

It untangled itself
and sang again
It danced and dances
with the wind

THINGS SHE IS NOT

No Fainting Daisy
No Helpless Hosta
No Wilted Bluebell
No Fightless Black-Eyed Susan
No Sinking Lily
No Thin Skinned Wallflower
No Shrinking Violet
No Sheepish Sundrop
No Damsel Desert Rose
No Soft Petal
No Thirsty Flower

ROCKABYE MAYBE

Mother Moon of harvest
Mother Moon of stone
Mother moon of tide
Moon rock in our bone
Mother moon of sharp tongue
Garlic wreath and fang
Moon of desperation
Light from which we came
Mother moon of blood flow
Moon of doe and fox
Mother moon, the ceiling
Orbiting sleepwalk
Mother moon your guidance
Ebbs and flows in waves
Bloodclot lunar crescent
Waning gibbous phase
Mother moon of troubles
Take our offerings
Two pinecones and a petal
As you
Unclip our wings

MIDWEST SUNSET

One by one
cars slow
and come to a stop
on the side of highways
and country roads
Red barns turned salmon
silhouettes
Passengers exit
their vehicles
and gaze in collective awe
We
Step out of the car
one foot at a time
The elderly set down
their forks in nursing homes
and gather at the window
Steamfitters take off their gloves
and lift their chins
Safety glasses reflecting
cyclists soaring down hills
to return home splashed with color
Students set down their homework
and study the sky
Each of us pausing momentarily
to feed our sadness to the setting sun
Eyes met with hope
on the horizon

DOE, A DEAR

I watch my feet like a black and white movie
dance across the porcelain, spread all my toes
Could be anyone's toes, they are not mine today

I soak to heal in the tub, black waffle shower curtain
closed and consuming, turns the cream surroundings
a grim and foggy gray
Feet translucent, water rusty jug

One exception, the Old Spice Bottle
Which appears in this light, doe blood drying on
                              a terry cloth rag

I want to close my eyes and imagine the
doe serene in her passing, bed of baby's breath,
crown of jasmine, silk ribbons hang on branches

*I want to close my eyes and hover above her ever so
slightly*

It is snowing, cardinals have gathered
    I close my eyes

Static.

WHO COOKS FOR YOU

The earth
smells like
thawed
dog shit
but I cook
my skin
in the sun
baking freckles
into my nose
as the worms
create spring
turd casseroles
and the birds
behead the worms
to feed their young
And the birds ask,
"Who cooks for you?"
And I answer
by raising
my carrot
to the sky,
Singing,
Whip-poor-will!
Whip-poor-will!
Cacaw
Chicka dee
dee dee dee
Cheep Cheep
Beep Beep
Skraww
And finally
Inquire,
"Who? Who?"

Made in the USA
Middletown, DE
28 December 2018